AF581989

HOW TO LOVE A CHEATING PARTNER WITHOUT CHEATING

PATHWAY TO A PEACEFUL RELATIONSHIP/MARRIAGE

Teryila Gerrard Anyam

Copyright © 2022 Teryila Gerrard Anyam

All rights reserved.

ISBN: 9798352883112

DEDICATION

This book is dedicated to my lovely parents Rev./Atese P.T. Anyam, PhD and all the wonderful parents out there who have dedicated their lives in keeping a peaceful home for their children.

CONTENTS

INTRODUCTION

Introduction A good marriage and a healthy relationship is the best gift a couple will enjoy from his or her partner. Nevertheless, there are many reasons such as distance, money, toxic behaviors, and many more that can take away a good marriage/relationship that one ought to have enjoyed. Many of these behaviors or characters can be accommodated in a relationship or marriage, especially when the other partner is an understanding person. There is this one very character that is hard to cope with in marriages and relationships.

When a partner has this character, it becomes a big issue to the other partner. Not only does it threaten the peace of marriage or relationship, but it also leads to depression, disappointment, heartbreak and sometimes it can even lead to death either by heart attack or suicide; Cheating. Many marriages and relationships are broken today as a result of cheating. When it comes to cheating, even the best of lovers become enemies and best of partners become strangers. Cheating hurts, cheating brings pains, unending sorrows especially when it's someone you so much love.

Many partners have ended their marriages and relationships because of cheating, there are still many who still truly love their partners even with the fact that they are cheating. The most painful part of cheating is what I do call 'double cheating.' Double cheating is when you know that your partner is cheating on you but you on the other hand can't cheat back probably due to the love you have on your partner and cannot stand another partner, at this point, many people feel double cheated; 1. Their partners are cheating on them. 2. They know they are cheating but they in turn cannot cheat.

You will believe with me that many lovers or couples out there today are experiencing the sting of double cheating. If you are such a person that truly loves your partner but he/she is cheating on you but you still love your partner, then this book is all for you. If you are married and your partner has been cheating but you still want to protect your marriage/family, maybe for the sake of your children then read page by page of this book. You are in a relationship that you have so much invested in and hoping that it will lead to marriage but it's been threatened by the cheating nature of your partner, don't worry, take a little time seat and relax, for here is the right tool that will fix that relationship.

The solution to your painful marriage is just some readings away from you. One big thing about this book is that, not only will it teach you how to love your cheating partner without cheating back but it will educate you on things that you can do as a partner in a relationship/marriage that will hopefully take away infidelity in your marriage/relationship.

A SAD STORY

A relationship or marriage can suffer a lot of wounds that gets healed with time, but one that takes longer time and even forever to heal is cheating. There is nothing as painful as learning that your partner is cheating on you especially when you have been so faithful in the marriage or relationship. Here is a sad-short story of an African woman who gave everything into her marriage from day one but got cheated by her husband yet she could not stand the reality of sleeping with another man. The story will help us to understand this book much better. For the sake of this book, I will be referring to her as 'African woman'.

African woman got married to her husband as a virgin in her early teens. Her husband was the one that deflowered her after their marriage. Before the marriage a lot of people had warned her not to marry the man on the ground that the husband to be was not a good person for her. She loved her husband so much that she still insisted on marrying him. She was reliable told that her husband to be was a chronic womanizer, a lot of women have turned down his marriage proposal due to his womanizing lifestyle. But due to the love and possibly the pressure from the family and the inexperience from a young lover, African woman still went ahead with the marriage.

The marriage was not as smooth as she expected it to be even though God blessed them with good children. African woman, with all the love she had on her husband and the innocent love she brought into her husband's house this did not stop her husband from doing what he was known of. In the early stage of their marriage, he tried to hide his lifestyle from her but as time went on, things started unveiling. It was no longer news to African woman that her husband was cheating on her. At first, she found it hard to believe due to the fact that it could be a mare propaganda or misjudgment of people on her husband. But reality hit her so hard in the face on the day she came back very late at night and discovered that her husband was with another woman on their matrimonial bed.

This was the beginning of pains and sorrow in the life of African woman. When she tried to complain, her husband got angry and wanted beating her up. Thanks to her children who stood there helplessly watching and trying to intervene. Their presence and pathetic act prevented the man from beating up his wife. But from that day onward things got worst and worst for African woman. The fear and respect that her husband used to have on her was no longer there, he does his things openly as if he was not married, he will make phone calls to his lovers in front of his wife not minding the emotional damage he was putting her in. On several occasions, African woman reported to different people and bodies within her husband's circle to help on the situation and turn things around but all her efforts proved abortive.

When her children became matured, they thought they will be able to control their father and bring back the cool atmosphere of marriage but it was obvious the man was not ready to change. With everything that was happening; the pressure from her friends to get someone that will love her and treat her right, someone that will give her the desired peace of mind, African woman stood her ground and stayed with her husband and children for over thirty years (30) of marriage. The striking part of the story that was very sympathetic was the fact that African woman new only her husband sexually as a man. All the years of her struggle and pains, she still never allowed another man, under no reason whatsoever, to have sexual knowledge of her. She stuck to her husband and kept her marital vowels.

How many partners will be able to withstand the pressure of a cheating husband and never cheat? Few or even none, right? But African woman did it, she proved that she was a strong woman, because of her faithful attitude she has kept the family together till date. She has built her children under her own watch and she is always proud that she never for once compromised. But how was African woman able to achieve this? With all the pains and the lies, the arguments and even fights, she still showed undiluted love to her cheating partner without cheating. This book will teach and explain to you the 'how' that African woman used to be able to achieve this height; loving her husband, not cheating, and been a good exemplary mother to her children.

Read the book till the end without missing any chapter or page in order not to miss out on all the important points and facts that made African woman to love her cheating husband without cheating

CHEATING IN MEN

When we speak of cheating or infidelity, we are referring to the act of one spouse or partner being unfaithful to a spouse or other partner. This occurs when another partner is sexually or at a point even romantically involved with another person other than his/her partner or spouse. In the process, promises are been broken.

It has been a general believe by the larger proportion of the society that men cheat more than women do. One might go as far as blaming nature for the cheating ability of men. Even when men are so satisfied in a relationship, they still find a reason to cheat on their partner, why? A man once said that men are like an open sea that can never be satisfied with water, fill the thousands of jars in the sea and it will still accommodate it. Give a man everything and he will still see a reason to find another woman attractive. Be the most beautiful woman on earth yet your man will still see a reason to admire another woman's beauty. Be the most hardworking wife on earth yet your partner will still appreciate the little work of another woman out there that he finds attractive. Is this true?

It is very easy for a man to cheat; this could be as a result of mother-earth (nature). Nature has made it in such a way that, growing up especially in the African concept boys are the ones to ask out a lady on a date. It will come to a point of competition among boys on the number of girls they have asked out and how many have accepted their request. They then come back to gist among themselves and celebrate their so-called records. This to them brings about respect and high esteem. Sometimes it will go to a point of such group of boys taking records of girls they have had sexual knowledge with.

I still remember sometimes back in our early youth, some of my friends had this competition among themselves to take record of girls they have had sex with and the first to reach 50 different sexual partners will be respected. Each time they have sleep with a girl they will go and record her name against the number she is on the list and then bring it to the table for round discussion. This automatically made them cheaters as they were involved with different partners at the same time. Been in a game or not one thing that was sure was that, they cheated on their partner and caused them pains.

So, imagine that this group of boys grows up with such mind set then how sure are you that they will remain faithful with their spouse or partners? They say that attitude develops over time and if this holds to be true then guys that grow up dating different girls will be and always remain cheaters even in their marriages if not for special intervention. With this in mind one can boldly say that nature has made men cheaters even from childhood.

Another point that comes into play when you talk about cheating on the side of men is polygamy. Many people have stated that men polygamous in nature. In the African settings and other parts of the world, men are entitled to many wives as he can but women are mostly restricted to just a single man. There are ancient stories of men that were recorded that had more than a single wife yet they were seen and been pointed to as noble men. King Solomon for example, had about 700 wives that were all married to him but hardly will you come across a woman that has attend this fit. When a woman knows more than a single man in marriage then such a woman is been considered as a prostitute.

With this it's clear that men cheat sometimes deliberately hiding under the canopy that culture or nature has made it so. Many at times I seat and wonder why this has to be so. Why will men grow up with this life of been so infidel to their partners? What is that thing that makes a man to admire a lady so much, dedicate all his efforts in making that woman to love and accept him then still turns around to cheat on that same woman? You might have your reasons for these answers but one reason I see to be so real and unique is the issue of high sexual attraction. Over a number of percentages of men that cheat out there is as a result of high sexual attraction, a man gets easily sexually attracted to the opposite sex. A man (not all but a meaningful number of them) has this inside feeling that when his sees an opposite sex he then fancies the possibility of having canal knowledge with that woman.

A man will be with a woman that he truly loves and cares for but that will not stop him from thinking about another woman he sees on the road that looks attractive or beautiful. Not that such a man wants to cheat but naturally he starts admiring another woman even when he is with his lovely partner or wife. The only thing that stands between him and the other woman is 'self-control'. Ones this self-control is no longer there, the man starts planning and making arrangements within him on how to get in touch with the woman that has caught his attention, which of course will eventually lead to him cheating on his partner or wife in a near feature.

Many at times men cheat and believe it's their right to cheat. A man will not only cheat on a woman but will boldly claim the woman has no right to grown over such act of his. In the ancient days in Africa, we had some part of African tradition that a man will bring his concubine over to his house and his legitimate wife will leave the bed, go and stay with her children or somewhere else and give the man the chance to have time overnight with the other woman on her matrimonial bed. When such a woman tries to complain or groan over this act, the man will not only beat her up but will of course send her away or marry another woman to replace her or punish her. He will come out clear that he is entitled to marry as many wives as he can after all it is his house, not minding the effect or emotional trauma he has put his own partner in. But a woman dares not tries it. Solomon with 700 wives still hand 300 concubines.

Religious wise, there are so many religious believe out there that give men the liberty to cheat on women and make it official. Some religion allows a man to marry and still have affairs with other women outside his marriage. Others can go as far as sending the legitimate wife parking in order to create room for another woman to whom he wants to marry. They will marry a certain number of wives and when they still want to add another wife, exceeding the religious required number, the man will marry off one of his wives in order to pave way for a new wife he wants to take in. The wives have little or no say in this.

With all this in mind I come to agree with the saying that 'men are naturally cheaters. Biologically (arguably though) men are born to cheat when compare to women. Men have this cheating lifestyle right from when they are born but the only thing that keeps some men from cheating is self-control over lost.

Another point out of the many that I will like to mention in this book about cheating in men is that of sexual satisfaction. There are many reasons that a man who wants to cheat will cheat on, but one of the striking reasons that many men cheat due to, even the most of men is that of sexual satisfaction. When a man finds sexual satisfaction outside his partner then be rest assured that such a man will always find his way back into the arms of that woman. It will now take a miracle for that man to forget about the sex experience he had out there. At this point the man seems to easily forget about every good thing that his partner has been doing for him and runs to the other woman at any slightest opportunity.

Even with this, I still have some reservations on the side of men, because if you are so faithful to your wife then what made you to have a test of another woman out there that you have come to know that she satisfies you in bed more than your own partner? That is the reason why it's advisable for people to choose partners that are so compatible in all ramifications. Learning is not bad. So, if you are a woman and you happen to be in love with a man that has this cheating desire in him and you still love him so much and don't want to lose him, at the same time you don't want to cheat on him as well then what exactly will you do? Read on, the solution to your problem is just minutes away from you.

CHEATING IN WOMEN

Just like men women also cheat. But some of the reasons to which they cheat differ from those of men. Nature has also played a good one when it comes to cheating on the side of women, it is very hard for a woman to cheat but at the same time, it is very easy for a woman to cheat. Complicated right? I will break it down for you.

What I mean by been very hard for a woman to cheat is; a woman does not easily get attracted to a man and even when she does nature has made it that it's very difficult for her to express her feelings towards that man. Unlike men who when they see what they love they go after it, women, even seeing what they love, they still have to wait, most at times for that which they love to make the first attempt. And if that attempt is not made by the opposite sex, then in most cases the feelings will disappear in due time without anything coming out of it. A woman is being created to control much of her feelings, feelings that will result into cheating. In a short term, a woman has more self-control than a man.

Another reason that makes a woman a hard cheater is love. A woman generally is a loving creature; she has the mind to love as long as she feels comfortable. There is this famous saying that 'when a woman loves, she loves with everything on her'; but pray that the love never turns into hatred. A woman who truly loves her partner will go extra miles to maintain that love and to preserve it. When she loves, she loves with all her might and soul. She loves like it's the end of the world. A woman can sacrifice anything for the love she shares especially when it's bringing in joy and happiness. During one of my heated arguments with a friend about football he stated that there are three people in this life that are difficult to convince and one among them is a woman that is in-love. This implies that, if a woman is truly in-love with a man, it will take more than ordinary effort for you to break that love.

Another point that heightened the self-control ability of a woman over a man is that of nature. I always say this to the girls around me; the pride of a woman is when she plays hard to get; like limiting guys' access to her. If you are a woman and you stick around with many men and have been involved with them, then you have lost a huge part of your pride. For sure you will be a round table discussion at one joint or the other. But the pride of a man is when he can have access to any girl he wants at any time. Before you crucify me over my assertion then I think you should blame nature, for it has made it so. Therefore, a woman that is in-love with a man and have developed this concept of 'a woman been hard to get' will make it so difficult for any man to convince her to cheat on her lover.

The second part of my statement that says 'it's easy for a woman to cheat' is due to the fact that a woman is vulnerable. Nature has exposed women to been chased by different men at the same time. A girl will be in a relationship or even in marriage, but due to nature, men will still be rushing after her, professing their love on her and even requesting and persuading her to have an affair with them. Rarely will you see this happening to a man. Men will go as far as throwing all their efforts towards that lady or woman to ensure they get what he wants. At this point a woman that has self-control will be at the verge of losing that especially when her relationship is not going smooth. At a point She will be carried away due to the level of persuasion and disturbances.

Another point that makes a woman an easy cheater is that, women love fancy things and nature has made them to be highly emotional about material things. When love and money are put together a woman's sense of reasoning start having partial contact. Displaying love and money to a woman to choose is like holding a banana on one side and plantain on the other side and asking a monkey to make a choice. Of course, we all know that monkey loves banana but due to the presence of the plantain and their look-alike appearance, it gives the monkey a difficult choice of selection, that monkey will prefer to go for both of the fruits. This is exactly what many women do out there. They want love but because of the display of money that can acquire their material things and afford their fantasies, it will leave a woman with no other option than to cheat by holding on with the man with true love and still not letting go the man with money.

Just like unsatisfied sex has been stated to be the major reason for men to cheat in a relationship or marriage, emotional dissatisfaction is the major reason in women. A woman will be able to cope with sexual dissatisfaction when love is involved without her cheating. I have personally seen marriages where the woman hardly have sexual satisfaction from her husband but still sticks around the marriage without cheating since the man is given her all the emotional satisfaction (comfort) she needs. One thing for sure is that, even the best of women out their will look somewhere else or will be tempted to ones they start experiencing emotional dissatisfaction from their partner. A woman generally hates it when her emotions are been toyed with, she starts feeling unsecured with the thought of another woman taking her position. She will have much love and respect on a man but at a point where she feels there is something you are doing to her and using her love (emotions) to cover-up, that love will automatically grow into hatred. At this point the woman starts exploring her chances by looking somewhere else where her emotions will be satisfied.

There is this funny joke that complements my claims above about the top reason women and men cheat. Men likes what they see (which leads to sexual thoughts), so women spend their time making up to bring a man to the table of sexual urge while on the other end, women like emotional satisfaction so men spend their time lying to them very well in order to satisfy their emotions and keep them under control. This clearly explains the top reasons while men and women cheat.

DANGERS IN CHEATING

There is a saying that some things are easily said rather than done. This adage holds true when you speak about loving a partner that you know very well cheats; it is easy to say but it's hard to be done. It is so easy to love a cheating partner and to be with him or her even in marriage if you are also a cheater. A relationship is so lovely if both partners are faithful to themselves or if both are cheating. But in a situation where one cheats and the other does not, it becomes a thug of war that sometimes led to the end of the relationship. Sometimes a particular partner might not have the mind to cheat but the moment he learnt that the other partner is cheating then things start changing. Cheating becomes an issue of deliberation. Revenge sets in.

The pains of a cheating partner are almost near to death. It hurts so bad that it can sometimes not really take the love away but give the other partner a misbehaving spirit that will push him/her to do things that such a person did not intend to do. In the case of African woman, she had to live with her husband for over 30 years knowing that he was cheating on her. Many people would have planned on taking revenge or taking away the life of the husband. Yes, you heard me right; partners do kill because of cheating. But the question is; is revenge, killing or any other nasty thing you do the best solution for a cheating partner? Yes, I will accept with you that there are certain things that one does to get inner peace especially taking revenge, but is cheating your life style? Were you waiting for an opportunity for you to cheat on your partner?

At this point one will be asking what is wrong for you to cheat back when your partner was the first to cheat. You might be right to cheat, after all, he/she started it first, your trust was betrayed, yes, but before you decide to take revenge by cheating on your partner, I will like you to listing to the dangers of cheating. One of the hardest things you will ever live with is the act of cheating (especially when you are not a cheater and you have conscience). When you cheat on your partner, conscience alone won't allow you to be free, constantly it will keep bringing you back to the reality that you have had an affair outside your relationship or marriage, your conscience will keep hunting you down. This guilty conscience is capable of sending you into depression that is worse than been cheated on.

In many cases, when your partner cheats on you and you want to take revenge on him, at that point your mind and thoughts are not right so you might end up having an affair with someone you never planned to, someone you never loved or won't have considered for a second. On realization of your act, it will be too late to reverse the decision. One funny thing is that the person to whom you were involved with might even comeback for more and at this point you will realize that you have made one of the greatest mistakes of your life.

There was a lady that was so angry when she caught her boyfriend with another woman in bed. She could not stand the fact that her boyfriend just cheated on her, her anger led her into having an affair with a man that week. All of them went their separate ways. Later on, the boyfriend came back and apologies to the lady and they both settled out. But after three years they both decided to get married, it was at this point that the girl realized that the man she had cheated on her boyfriend with three years ago on in the name of revenge was actually her boyfriend's uncle. The guilt, the feelings and the shame almost denied this girl of her expected marriage. To worsen the situation, the stupid uncle wanted a continuation of that single act all in the name of he can't forget it. This is what anger of cheating can cause. This is one of the consequences of a cheating revenge; getting involved with someone you never would have considered but due to anger you end up with the person. Of course, you can imagine how this marriage will be for this lady, having someone you have had an affair with in the family and is still requesting for more.

Another thing an angry partner who wants to get revenge on her cheating partner should know is; sex is not just an act but just more of soul ties. When you sleep with different partners you tie your soul with them, their souls may come in different forms of darkness. Some of those souls could possibly destroy you or delay your blessings. A soul that you sleep with in the name of revenge might be capable of destroying your marriage or your relationship. When you go about sleeping with different partners in order to get back at your partner that has just cheated on you, know that your body has different shadows consisting of different souls, you are not you, but a single body been entire to different souls.

Another notable consequence of cheating which is familiar to many people is that of health risk. When you are involved with different partners the more you increase your chances of having sexual transmitted diseases. You will think and be sure about using protection when you cheat, yes; it's advisable but how secured are you? There are certain health challenges that are not necessarily transmitted with the act of sex, sometimes you can contact these diseases due to intimate contact with such an affected person, the act of kissing, the act of sharing things together, the exchange of sweat during a protective sex and many more are all the risk you stand when you are involved with another partner that you are not too sure of.

So, before you take that revenge of cheating on your partner you should know that the person you are going to get involve with might also have someone aside from you. You can take all the precaution measures to ensure that your cheating mate too is clean but you are not sure about the other partner that he/she is been involved with. You cannot completely control the life of that person you are cheating with especially when he/she knows that you are married or in another relationship. So that person can still be involved with other people and still come back to have sex with you exposing you to all the risk that you have been avoiding and been careful all your life. The sure way to keep yourselves out of the danger of infectious disease of this nature is to be faithful with each other. One may ask that what if am been faithful and my partner is cheating and exposing us to these same dangers that this book is warning about, what then should I do? Don't worry, that is why you are reading this book, it will tell you everything you need to do to counter such a situation without losing the love you have on your partner.

Another strong point I will like to pen down here specially to married couples is the psychological effect and consequences that cheating will have on the immediate family, especially on the children. Before you go out there to cheat or take a revenge on your cheating partner then you should for ones consider your children. Cheating directly or indirectly affect the children most in the family. When there is a cheating partner in the family, there are high chances of your own children copying up the lifestyle of their parents, when such a lifestyle is been copied or learnt over time then the children grow up with the mindset and knowledge of cheating which will affect their lives in a long run maybe when both the parents are old and their children start having their own families.

You as a parent might have cheated all your life but had little or no consequences of your actions but how sure are you that your child that have copied your cheating habit and had made it their own lifestyle will have the same grace that you have enjoyed? This will lead to broken marriages for your children, assault and disgrace that you in your old age will not be comfortable with, but the fault will be on you. There are more than 75% chances that a cheating family or relationship will have no peace. In this type of family there is always arguments and quarrel between the husband and the wife, sometimes there is even physical fight among the couples (like in the case of the African woman), this shameful act can even happen in the presence of the children leading to psychological effect, either emotionally or mentally. It pushes these children out of the comfort of their homes, exposing them to all sort of social vices and criminal effects out there. Early marriages, unwanted pregnancy, sexual abuse victim, stealing, and many more are the product of children who grow up in a cheating and unstable home.

This without doubt will lead to the end of your peaceful and dreamful marriage. It will lead to a broken home with the children either taking the side of the mother or the father or sometimes even growing up to hate both parents. This brings enmity not just among the partners but also among the children and brings about conflict in the family that can last even beyond the marriage. It even gets worst when the children are divided; others been on the side of the father while others are supporting the mother, they both start hating each other. This will lead to everlasting dispute that will cut across many generations even when the direct culprits to the act (cheating) have long been dead and buried.

So now that you have learnt of the dangers and consequences in cheating and revenge cheating to both the partners and the people around them, I know that we need to be careful out there in dealing with our partners knowing that this will have a way more consequences that we have ever imagined. Another challenge left is; what if your partner cheats so much and does not want to stop, what then should you do? The answer to this question is the main point of this book which forms the next chapter.

LOVING A CHEATING PARTNER WITHOUT CHEATING

As earlier stated in the introductory part of this book, the hardest thing in love is coping with someone you truly love but is cheating on you. Cheating hurts so bad that you will feel the only way out is leaving the relationship. But like one man once said; 'leaving a cheating partner for another partner is like leaving Nigeria to USA because of rain; it rains everywhere, it also rains in the US. How sure and you that your new partner will not cheat? This is not in any way trying to encourage cheating but only making you understand that there is no guarantee that a particular person will not cheat. Now that we have come this far about cheating and double cheating, it is good for us to know the way out of this tough situation.

There is a popular saying that, a problem known is half solved. Now that we have already identified most of the consequences of cheating and cheating revenge in the previous chapter (read chapter five if you haven't) then the solution is half way solved. With those consequences alone, it will serve as a motivating point for any partner not to think of cheating or taking a revenge cheating. But rather concentrate on the possible way of making the relationship or marriage better. At this point I must warn that if you don't love your partner, this solution I am about to provide might not work for you. It a solution for those who truly love their partners and feel they have a feature with each other, while for couples it's a must read-solution for them.

The first step in dealing with a cheating partner is to accept the fact that your partner is cheating or has cheated. This is what kills, knowing the reality that your partner that you have owned all to yourself and have sacrificed everything for as the case might be, is not exactly what you thought he/she was, accepting this is not easy. The more you refused accepting this reality, thinking you are dreaming or living in fantasy world is the more it keeps eating you up and the thought of cheating keep tempting you. It is one thing to catch your cheating partner and another to accept that truly he/she has cheated. The benefit of accepting it is that you free your mind from the burden of over thinking. Secondly, when you accept this hurting act of cheating then it frees your mind to think about the way forward.

Accepting to the fact that your partner has cheated is like forgiving someone who has offended you. In this case, the more you refuse to forgive someone who has wronged you, the more you think and carry a lot of burden in your heart and hinders your ability to think right especially each time you see that person. Same is applicable to accepting the reality of a cheating partner, the earlier you accept it the earlier the killing-thoughts and feelings disappears, but the more you hold and keep on thinking that it is not true, it's a dream, it's not your partner, etc., the more it keeps on hurting you and making you to think of things that are not right. So, first step is accepting the fact that it has happened and nothing that you will do that will reverse the act.

The second step you need to do when your partner is cheating is to know his reasons. Yes, you heard me right. Even though there is no justification whatsoever for a partner to cheat on another but if you love your marriage or your relationship and wants to save it from collapsing then you have to take this step after you have accepted the fact that your partner has cheated. Try to know the reason why your partner did that. It might be annoying but at this point your partner (the cheater) in most cases is vulnerable and has the chances of telling you the reason(s) for his or her actions. But in many situations the cheater might even be ignorant of what he has done like in the case of African woman. At this point the person might be even ready to fight or beat you up for questioning him. So, you need to be calm and cool in order to make him/her open up to you in details.

Knowing his reasons will help you to know how to tackle it and probably overcome the situation and prevent feature reoccurrence. Who knows, you might even be the reason for your partner's cheating act. But you have to know that at this point none of these steps will work again if you are not able to forgive your partner. You must, at this point (if you have not done it) forgive your partner in order to tackle his/her reasons of cheating on you. Know that this will only work when you are ready to help the person, it can never be a one-sided battle, collectively you must work towards doing it. Sounds wild right? I want you to understand that cheating in most cases is like addiction that takes more than ordinary efforts to quit even when there is a desire to quit. When someone is addicted to a particular thing, he/she might want to quit doing it due to reasons but it will be more difficult to do it. Same is applicable to cheating. It needs more than ordinary efforts to kill the act of cheating especially when it has been developed over time.

You might ask that was it a collective effort that made your partner to cheat? The answer of course is no, it was not a collective effort. The next question will be then why is it that in sorting it out it has become a collective effort? This is because you want to save your marriage or your relationship. Remember that I told you that the solution to loving a cheating partner only works for those who truly love their partners. It is possible that your partner might have made up his mind and swear all his gods with you never to cheat again, but if you don't play along, the same act will still repeat itself and you won't blame your partner entirely. Remember that your primary aim is to save your marriage and the person your partner cheated on out there will be doing everything possible to ensure that the two of them are still together, that is why collectively you have to help your partner to fight off this intruder that wants to reap where he/she did not sow.

Many will be thinking now that even if I cheat back on my partner that will not stop me from helping my partner. Yes, you can cheat back on your partner in order to get back at him or even just to satisfy your conscience in order to stay put in your relationship or marriage. You can actually do this without the knowledge of your partner or do it for your partner too to be hurt and of course if your partner loves you that much, he/she will be hurt. There is what is known as 'a feeling of intense guilt' which if you know of you will not try to cheat on your partner because your partner has cheated on you.

The level of extreme guilt that you are going to face after you have taken a cheating revenge on your partner is what I believe that most people will not stand, especially when they love their partner that much. This extreme guilt tends to be even worse when you get away with the affair or one-night stand without being caught. In many cases it does not even go away simply because you have confessed back to your partner. Repressed guilt can also lead to a whole bunch of side effects that you might not be able to stand. Are you then ready to take a revenge that will take the joy of your life away?

Another step in loving your cheating partner without cheating is for you to leave the poor cheater with his guilt. A secret you don't know about cheating is that, cheating hurts the cheater more than the victim. This is because of the health issues and personal anguish that can arise later on. Know that anxiety and depression that your cheating partner stands to get after cheating on you are both symptoms of repressed guilt, which can also manifest in other ways. Physically, someone that is struggling with guilt can experience insomnia and a loss of appetite. The shame of cheating can eat him/her up to the point where their lives become miserable. But the moment you cheat back you have given that person a reason to be vindicated by his/her conscience.

There was a time I was having a misunderstanding with my girlfriend, I tried to know the reason why she was angry with me and was acting strange. On several occasions I asked her to tell me her problems but she refused but keeps on making issues out of nothing. I was head cool, knowing that she wants a fight which I promise not to give her. On this faithful evening she called me when I was watching a match and I did not notice her four missed calls but as soon as I came out the viewing center, a strange number called and it was her, she hit back at me so hard without even hearing from me and when I tried to explain she said I was speaking rubbish. Three times she shouted rubbish to me, I got angry and said she was stupid for saying to me that my explanations are rubbish. What followed next was the guilt that I was having in my mind by returning insults back on her. On her side she felt vindicated because I insulted her back. That is exactly what happens when your partner cheats on you and then you cheat back to take a revenge. Not only do you take the guilt but your actions also exonerate that person and if care is not taken it will be the end of your marriage or relationship.

The above steps and consequences of revenge cheating are the solutions to your long-term problem. This is how you can show love or handle your cheating partner without cheating. Yet the punishment he will get will be far more than you cheating back to give him/her a point to prove. When these steps are followed rightly and the partners love themselves then the relationship/marriage will be as ever strong as before and even more. One good thing to know is the fear and respect your partner will have on you when he learnt that you have shown him/her nothing but love. Cheating and love are things you cannot keep away from each other but the moment you learn how to cope with both is the begging of a better relationship and marriage.

These were the secret to the over 30 years of African woman's marriage. She loved her husband endlessly but still her husband cheated and even try to beat her up but she kept to herself by been faithful to this man and in turn not only did she saved her marriage but she was a foundation to which her children and the entire family survived on. At the end the man realized his mistakes (even though it was a bit late) thanks to the above steps that African woman took and the consideration she had on the dangers of revenge cheating. Today her children call her a hero and she has become a role model not only to her children but the society at large. This is how to love a cheating partner without cheating.

ABOUT THE AUTHOR

Teryila Gerrard Anyam popularly known as 'D Young Captain' is a zealous youth that is so concern about the norms and practices of the society. He believes in a peaceful and egalitarian society.

Nigerian by nationality, Tiv by tribe, he holds the dream that the world can actually be a better place. This can be achieved by touching individual lives and families.

The good thing about this book is that its non-fictional which makes it practicable.

www.ingramcontent.com/pod-product-compliance
Lightning Source LLC
LaVergne TN
LVHW021350160826
845679LV00008B/1564

* 9 7 9 8 3 5 2 8 8 3 1 1 2 *